Everyone's Alone Tonight

Poems by

James Benger and Jason Baldinger

Kung Fu Treachery Press
Rancho Cucamonga, CA

Copyright © James Benger, Jason Baldinger 2019
First Edition 1 3 5 7 9 10 8 6 4 2
ISBN: 978-1-950380-42-8
LCCN: 2019943093

Design, edits and layout: John T. Keehan, Jr.
Cover and title page images: Jonathan Dowling
Author photos: Hannah Benger, Ethan Meyer
All rights reserved. No part of this publication may be reproduced or transmitted in any form or by any means, electronic or mechanical, including photocopying, recording or by info retrieval system, without prior written permission from the author.

Praise for James Benger and Jason Baldinger:

"In Everyone's Alone Tonight the characters within have learned the hard way to expect little from life. This collection is a series of sharp-eyed accounts covering "…the volatile acts of free-falling humans…" People are spiritually isolated, fenders are rusty, towns are small and jobs are dead-end or nonexistent. Small pleasures can be found in the warm light of a run-down corner bar or in a solitary room, listening to a turntable spinning a scratched and popping record that was a favorite in years past.

In these pieces, James Benger and Jason Baldinger share an effective economy of phrasing- "Brant was raised by his Grandma, she of the glass eye and the whomping cane…"- as we follow their narrators attempting to navigate a crooked road that has often been passed from generation to generation.

Authentic is an overused word these days but these poems ring true, bringing to mind the great work of poet Don Winter and the prose of Daniel Woodrell.

With Everyone's Alone Tonight, Benger and Baldinger survey the disconnected people and places that too often are invisible in this clever-quipping perfect-selfie age. Haunting and heartfelt, this is a book to be savored."

-Curtis Hayes, author of *Bottleneck Slide- Poems*

"sifting the rubble of a long-dying, but not quite dead yet town of pickup trucks and chew." These lines by Benger describe the world these two poets walk perfectly. Poems about small towns the sad stories the raw nerve it takes to see the art in these lives is what gives these poems their unique power. Baldinger and Benger write them like they lived them. In Postcards from Jeanette Pennsylvania Baldinger writes "maybe that's just how it is when you watch another version and another version and another version of your life crumble" These are powerful poems starring the lost, the lonely, the hard-working everyman/woman. These are poems for all of us because they are about all of us."

-Matthew Borczon author of *A Clock of Human Bones.*

"This is Americana from the "Middle". Poems written by 'working hands' "...sifting the rubble of a/ long-dying". Poetry, "For Tammy at the Wal Mart Tire & Lube". Postcards from those places we don't want to admit we've been. Places we can't stop visiting. Places we might still be living in."

-Huascar Medina, Poet Laureate of Kansas, author of *How to Hang the Moon*

Some of these poems have appeared in *I 70 Review, Things Have Changed, Winedrunk Sidewalk, Gasconade Review, Rustbelt Review, Mojave River Review, Cajun Mutt Press, Outlaw Poetry, The Rye Whiskey Review, Alien Buddha Zine, Fixator Press, Rasputin* and *As It Ought To Be.*

Also by James Benger:

The Park (2019 Aldrich Press)
Against The Dark (with Tyler Robert Sheldon)
    (2019 Stubborn Mule Press)
Things Have Changed (2019 Dark Particle Press)
Little Fires Hiding (2018 Kung Fu Treachery Press)
You've Heard It All Before (2017 GigaPoem)
As I Watch You Fade (2016 EMP)
Jack Of Diamonds (2013 LAB 52)
Flight 776 (2012 LAB 52)

Also by Jason Baldinger:

The Whiskey Rebellion (with Jerome Crooks) (Six Gallery Press)
The Lady Pittsburgh (Speed & Briscoe Press)
The Studs Terkel Blues (NightBallet Press)
The Lower Forty-Eight (Six Gallery Press)
Fragments of a Rainy Season (Six Gallery Press)
Fumbles Revelations (Grackle and Crow)
This Useless Beauty (Alien Buddha Press)
The Ugly Side of the Lake (with John Dorsey) (NightBallet Press)
Little Fires Hiding (2018 Kung Fu Treachery Press)
The Better Angels of Our Nature (Stubborn Mule Press)

TABLE OF CONTENTS

In This Town / 1

Wonderbread, Chipped Ham, Tastycakes / 3

Junkyard / 6

Postcard from Jeanette Pennsylvania / 8

After the Railyard / 10

Beckemeyer Illinois 1958 (for Roy Beckemeyer) / 12

Corners / 14

Postcard from Harman West Virginia / 15

Etiquette / 16

Sandstone Weathered (for Alyssa Trivett) / 18

Outset / 20

New Eagle Pennsylvania 1960 / 21

Brant / 23

Northside 1982 (for Richard Cronborg) / 26

Forecast / 28

For Tammy at the Wal-Mart Tire and Lube / 29

Everyone's Alone Tonight / 31

The View from Finzel / 33

Middle / 35

A Palomino and a Bull Snake (for Linzi Garcia) / 36

Documents / 37

1965 Vintage Tape Hiss / 39

Loss / 41

Dead Flowers / 42

Lower / 44

Duke's Upper Deck Cafe / 45

Nothing / 46

A River on Fire / 48

Mr. Petty / 50

Beauty is a Rare Thing / 53

Rot / 56

Postcard from a Sunday Morning / 58

Shelter / 60

The Ballad of Dominic Ierace / 62

Cross-Dimensional / 64

For Endless Summer / 66

Sliver / 68

Lee's Famous Fried Chicken / 70

Life / 71

This Drunk Apparition / 75

today / 78

Midnight Prayer / 79

*I never saw my hometown
until I stayed away too long.*
>— Tom Waits
>From *San Diego Serenade*

*I've worked for the rich,
I've lived with the poor.
I've seen many a heartache,
there'll be many more.
I've lived luck and sorrow,
been to success and stone.
I've endured,
I've endured.
How long can one endure?*
>—Ola Belle Reed

In This Town

In this town
the whores trade war stories
with the cops
down in front of the smoke shop.

Neon lights proclaiming
XXX
are a beacon of civility.

An abandoned Buick
on the highway to the suburbs
is only another reminder
of the temporary nature of existence.

The guys down at the bar
tie another one on
while their children
figure out life.

A blue-eyed dog
searches the back alleys
for his next or his last meal.

Money changes hands
like a forgotten promise,

while tomorrow's score
is a technicolor dream.

Some silent flapper show
plays at the movie house,
but the tape is a bad dub
and the girls dance to
more hiss than jazz.

In this town
the gutters flow freely
and the rivers run dry
and every one of us
couldn't imagine
life any other way.

-Benger

Wonder Bread, Chipped Ham, Tastycakes

it's not a real road
until you see a front-end loader
pulled over, horse collared
at the roadside by a cop car
right near the ass
of a wal-mart

I honestly forgot
it was memorial day
until I hit the hill
the cemetery stretching
up festooned in hundreds
of flags, if there was a grave
to honor, you couldn't find
it in the wind here

in town the football players
are walking to their cars
token flags and shoulder pads

this town was a stop
on the underground railroad
the supermarket has specials
on wonder bread, chipped ham
and tastycakes. the food truck
serves funnel cake and sno-cones

the veterans hang
from light posts, the bunting
in the windows, we only give
lip service to our wars, maybe no
one needs to know what a just war is
maybe we don't want to look that close

if we cared more maybe
the pizza shop on 4th wouldn't
have closed so long ago
that the weeds are up to the window

if we cared more we'd
all have two busted ass trans-ams
parked on our quarter acre manicured lawn
maybe if we cared more
we could afford one of those
ranch houses on utopia street

instead we run for the hills
this parade healed
in that same elemental way
as a sunday church service
we take away our lies
our misconceptions that we swear
we're right about
hold them close
to our hearts

while we wait weeks
for rain to wash
the piles of horse shit
that were left by the corner
of walnut street away

-Baldinger

Junkyard

The grass was never so high
you'd worry too much about
stepping on glass
or snakes;
yellowed, thin and patchy,
it did little more than
add some color to the
cracked brown summer dirt.

There was an old school bus,
something from our parents' time,
the remains of a couple
non-descript sedans,
more decay than machine.
Not too far out in the woods
that lined the place,
there was most of the axles
and a couple steel hoops
that once framed canvass.
We imagined that
skeleton of a covered wagon
held the ghosts of secret lives,
and maybe we weren't that far off.

The sun baked white on
discarded faded plastic nothings
as we dubbed ourselves archaeologists;

sifting the rubble of a
long-dying,
but not quite dead yet
town of pickup trucks and chew.

We searched for anything that made sense;
anything that would tie it together,
tie our existence together,
knot it all into a tidy reason,
gift wrapped for our easy consumption.

We spent all summer
for a few summers
hunting those answers,
but all we ever really found was
strangers' trash and
a few rusted-out hulks to
jump around in.

But maybe that's enough;
maybe that's all we needed in the first place.

-Benger

Postcard from Jeanette Pennsylvania

there's a fight
outside the dollar general
somebody punched somebody
everybody was screaming
broken noses blossom

the party place
blares *happy birthday*
to an empty street

they sell bread
in the saint vincent depaul
day old or expired
for a quarter

everything here
costs a quarter
still, there's nothing
I want

there are
three Italian restaurants
around town, the waitress
smells like christmas

I can't tell if she was born in 1952
or she died in 1952
but she's still here

maybe that's just how it is
when you watch
another version
and another version
and another version
of your life
crumble

-Baldinger

After the Railyard

I've been in this basement apartment
in the West Bottoms since a few
wars ago. Several presidents ago.
Countless funerals ago. I've long
ago retired from the railyard. The
pension isn't great, but it's good
enough to keep me in food and this
little hole in my hometown.

Rain's coming down outside,
and a little inside.
It's warm enough. For me at least.

I'm under a blanket, in a chair that's
nearly as old as me. I've got a drink
in my hand, not top-shelf, but not
from the bottom either. Charlie Parker's
on the phonograph, reminding me
how it is. As if I could ever forget.
In my other hand, I've got a book by
someone from around here. Someone
who understands, who's been through
it all before. I've read the lines so many
times, I'm not actually reading anymore;
only reciting in my head things I've
always known.

It's been raining dark night and day for so long, I'm not quite sure I remember what the sunshine actually looks like. In fact, I'm not sure if it is night or day; I forget to wind my watch. A lot.

The rain's still coming, and I feel sleep coming to join it. Maybe this will be the last time.

-Benger

Beckemeyer Illinois 1958 (for Roy Beckemeyer)

we usually headed to Shoal Creek
once I got older, sometimes
it was Carlyle Lake
we'd find a dark alcove
toss our lines out from shore
sometimes we'd use a boat
listen while the bow cut the water
my father would tell us again
about how it was working in the mines
about everyone's brother or uncle gone
about the cave-in's, the explosions
about how they lost a hand, a leg
maybe if they we're lucky only a finger
if they weren't then maybe their lives
as I got older I took this as a reminder
to get out of town, to not let the mines
take me down and I listened

he would tell us again about our grandfather
a machine runner, how he was running
the air puncher when a ton of slate
came down on him, how it shattered his back
they dug him out and took him to St. Louis
but it was too late, he was gone

no matter how many times he told the story
the hair on my neck always stood up
the helmets we used these night
were taken out of the mines
I wondered then if the light
that shown above me
was the last light
my grandfather
had seen

-Baldinger

Corners

She finds corners to be the best.
No one bothers,
no one attacks,
no one talks,
offers help,
gives advice,
promises how good the world is
outside of the corner.

She finds corners to be the best.
Dark,
lonely,
claustrophobic
as they are,
they are hers,
and no one sees,
so no will
take them from her.

-Benger

Postcard from Harman West Virginia

she wears camo skirt
british flag t-shirt
waits tables
busses and cooks
in a seven table
four calendar restaurant
under the shadow
of a mountain
the woman
ahead pays, tips,
says, *you work hard*
buy yourself something nice;
a gift from jesus

                -Baldinger

Etiquette

There's only one urinal, one toilet,
and it never fails that
every time your back teeth
are really floating,
you're better off heading to the
alley out back.

I'm bleeding the dragon
against a frozen brick wall,
humid ammonia cloud
rising like the noxious smoke
from a fire at a munitions plant.

The scurrying in the dumpster
on the other side of the alley
I'd dismissed as rats turns out to be
a greying man, roadmap skin and
dull-to-the-point-of-dead eyes.

Some of the nicer patrons
will piss in used beer bottles
instead of using the wall.
They leave them lined up,
freezing to the pavement.

The man gets from the dumpster,
picks up a bottle, tips it to his mouth.
There's an equal chance it's beer,
or piss, or cigarette ash and spit.

I zip up and go back inside.

-Benger

Sandstone Weathered (for Alyssa Trivett)

I don't know how
but the wheels
are falling off
again
as usual
can't keep track
of how many times

standing on the shores
of the Chesapeake
holding my breath
against January
the smell of the ocean
alive, yet still
a distant memory

the eighteenth century
churchyard, sandstone
weathered unreadable

we creak
together
wobble unsure

my head collapsed
capsized under
the weight
of last night's drink

I woke up on a dorm room
floor, sleeping bag padding
against concrete. my spine
straight at least
it says/ does nothing
for my eyesight

is it Baltimore today?
what was last night
crashing between parties
atoms flowing predestined

the night almost ended
in a fistfight
that's not strange
anymore

proximity;
the effect
of the volatile
actions of free
falling humans
clinging
desperately
out of control

-Baldinger

Outset

A broken highway
is the only way.

Treads nearly new,
and a front seat
of possibilities
with every vehicle
coming from the distance.

The sky turns red
at the horizon.

He walks.

-Benger

New Eagle Pennsylvania 1960

he has a knack
for knowing
it's the hottest
day of the year

he comes home
from the mine
washes coal dust
from his face
his neck, his arms
changes into his
only pair of shorts

on his way
to the porch
he grabs
the beer
that's been
chilling for
over a year

he pops the top
sweat breaks
on his brow
coal dust mascara

runs down
his face

as long
as there's suds
in the bottle
he's completely free

-Baldinger

Brant

They'd try to pass off these
thin pieces of burnt bread
topped with a thin coat of
purple jellyish stuff
as breakfast for the kids
who had to be
dropped off early.
Later, they'd take the leftovers
(they were all leftovers),
call the hours-old crap
dessert in the lunchroom.

It was in that part of the line
where I'd meet Brant
every day.

Brant was perpetually greasy,
wore the same holey clothes
every day.
He had an eye that was always
looking somewhere else,
and equal love for
Guns N' Roses,
and the confederate flag.

I don't know why,
guess all it took was being civil,
and not a total dick to him,
he decided we were friends
for the brief minutes
every day
in the lunch line
where we received our toast.

Brant was raised by his grandma,
she of the glass eye
and the whompin cane.
Claimed his grandpappy was
higher-up in the
state militia.
Said the old man
would take him to
weekend drills
where he was treated royally.

One day in the lunch line,
Brant told me
any weekend, say the word,
he and his grandpappy,
they'd take me down there,
give me a rifle,
I can order those maggots around,
just like Brant.

I never believed much of anything
Brant said in our
daily minutes,
but one day he gave me
an Aerosmith tape,
just 'cause.
So that was pretty cool.

-Benger

North Side 1982 (for Richard Cronborg)

it was every bar in the North Side
long gone places like the 222 on Federal
the Rosa Villa on East General Robinson
a couple places lost in Spring Garden
the bar that burned down on Woods Run
that one that seemed darker than the rest
somewhere in the holler on Bascom
Riggs on Brighton somehow still stands

everyone knew my dad
in those places that hung heavy with hunkie smoke
those places of little hiding
those places of forgetting
those dark places with the rough comradery of men

they were always happy
to see my dad, he had a baggie
or a couple pills to palm
into some cash

we'd belly up the bar
he'd order a Stroh's
all the bartenders would laugh
as I climbed the stool
already seasoned

I'd order a Shirley Temple
a Roy Rogers, they may
muss my hair, say
you got a fine boy

these are the secrets
as they are, as they were
passed down from generations
sometimes from fathers to daughters
always from fathers to sons

-Baldinger

Forecast

She searches for
any semblance of
meaning.

Days are
drizzle-darkened pavement,
and the nights,
the flashing neon,
thundering rail lines
of anywhere and everywhere
else.

Tonight, the lightning strobes,
bone cracks outside
a forgotten window.

Tomorrow there may be sun.

-Benger

For Tammy at the Wal Mart Tire & Lube

Dan says it's an hour and a half
wait for an oil change
Dorsey and I walk perimeter
dream of snack bars
and people watching
we are out of luck though
this wal mart has random
park benches, but nowhere
to congregate

in the tire and lube
waiting area, like the bullpen
like we're handcuffed to desks
waiting to be taken in
for a line up, for intake
we make the best of it
telling road stories

her daughter dances
circles in newly purchased
light up sandals, Tammy
on the phone
tells someone that
they've been through
hell together, but they'll
make it through stronger

the attendant comes in
tells Tammy they can't patch
her tire, its more patch
now anyway, a new tire
is fifty-eight dollars, her
face sags, a broken heart
can't be patched, there
is no way left to stretch
when the bottom
closes in. Tammy's face
snaps, her voice breaks
as she toughens again
she claims there's nothing wrong
with the tire, they're trying to rip
her off, the attendant shakes
his head, this is a stalemate
where no one gets
an even break

-Baldinger

Everyone's Alone Tonight

There's too many people
alone here tonight.
Almost no conversation,
unless you count
waitresses and bartenders
angling for high-test tips.

The girl by the door,
she keeps making the move
like she'll leave as soon as
this last one is drained,
but the next one comes
before she can,
stuck in an endless loop of
just one more…

The old man at the bar
is more than hunched over
his infinitely refilling
shot and beer,
the way his head droops,
the liquid will outlast him.

The wiry man in the back booth
slowly nods his chin down to his chest,
bouncing back up,
barely touched pitcher vibrating
on the scarred table.

He shuffles to the can,
comes back a few minutes later
a new man,
runny nose, red eyes
and a can-do attitude.

Everyone in this place is alone tonight,
even the old man in the back room,
half-chewed cigar like some cartoon trope,
sorting the cash, the checks,
the crippling credit card receipts,

Everyone's alone tonight,
and this place won't fix it.

-Benger

The View from Finzel

the last time I remember
running into you and your ex
was outside my apartment
all of us drunk, three am
accidental meetings
we jumped the fence of daycare
next door. tried to fit
ourselves in tiny plastic houses
you wore a tiara
maybe we pretended to have tea
I remember we laughed ourselves blind

now with our last dance
a mirror of our first
it makes you wonder
if the matrix ran out of ideas
every day the same
only minor variants

tonight, in Finzel
quarter moon cottoned
in clouds. windmills
across the state line
blink intermittent red

I hang a right
after the welcome sign
route 160
weeks before
Labor Day
windows down
the night smells
like the death of summer

the lights of the next town
boil darkness to essentials

articulations
of the heart make
their own roadmap

flash to
Vancouver
a few years ago
snapping pictures of a sign

the first, cut off
maybe you fall in
the second
maybe you fall in love

-Baldinger

Middle

The truck is
more rust than red paint,
and the mutt in the bed
growls bloodthirsty.

Creaky doors and
blue smoke belches.

Ancient bug guts
decorate the
spiderwebbed windshield.

The driver's hat promises
a return to traditional values.

Cornfields outside the
passenger window
unravel.

-Benger

A Palomino and a Bull Snake (for Linzi Garcia)

there were four water towers on the Salina skyline
more than ten rooms with private baths in the place I stayed
I've lived the last couple days on gin and tequila
there's been no need to hit the brakes over the last eighty miles
it feels like I'm barnstorming a prairie fire

the longest train I ever saw was in Amarillo
that was before today, although it may have been Sheridan
Amarillo is four hundred miles south
Sheridan is a Palomino and a Bull Snake away

in the distance, there's a storm stuck over Topeka
I've seen so much big sky, empty plains
It makes me wanna swing north for the Badlands
I could make Rapid City by morning

yesterday, I learned that Mexican Buffet
are the two most perfect words in the English language
as I left, I noticed the only graffiti on the men's room wall
my asshole is burning
except both of the s's were faint, they had been corralled
to some Baptist ranch in the sky, where profanity
is still the devil's tongue

yesterday, I found I can turn bread crumbs into bluebirds
if I head north, gun it through Nebraska
I gonna try my luck turning motels into buffalo

-Baldinger

Documents

I would lie alone,
hours on end,
darkness swallowing
everything outside
that basement window.

Coyotes yipped in the field,
crying to a moon that
gave pale guidance
to all underneath.

Homemade 2X4 and plywood fame
cradling a yard sale
waterbed mattress,
a scavenged turntable,
rewired speakers,
soldier and superglue connections.

Look hard enough, you can find
records for fifty cents,
a dollar.
Many are missing jackets,
they all pop
and hiss,
and skip,

but deep in those
black oil grooves,
through those speakers that never
project every frequency
like they once did,
fallen heroes
speak through years.

-Benger

1965 Vintage Tape Hiss

there are Mellotrons
bursting from the car stereo
layered in 1965 vintage tape hiss

the last leaves of the season
rain down
street lights
strobe
I can feel my spine
everything shines

the city
still has
a hole in it

everyone sits
in the rapture
of attention

on stage
on a rug
sitting in
purple lights
someone plays
Christian Marclay's
Record Without A Cover
like 1985 was a time that mattered

I wonder
how many drug deals
are happening
right now

all I want is darkness
Theremin and Mellotron
to carry me in a moment

I want something like
perfection

something like
Good Vibrations

what was it?
pocket symphony?
teenage symphony to god?

what is it now?
middle age symphony
to what?

…

fading time
or
time faded

-Baldinger

Loss

Some days
she doesn't do anything;
is perfectly still in a
sterile world.
The reality of their world is a
perverse death wish.

She understands on all levels
exactly what she's wasting:
the day,
the light,
the world,
her life.

She knows this in the
most unsugarcoated way,
as an absolute truth,
but in the darkness,
on the floor,
with the noiselessness
of a non-existence
throbbing in her weary veins,
she doesn't see any of it
as all that much of a loss.

-Benger

Dead Flowers

she requests a walk in the cemetery
she got flowers for her birthday
a first, she's held onto them too long
now she wants to leave
dead flowers
a gift on some random grave

dead flowers rest in a paper bag
we drain our beers
start walking

inside the gate
I ask if she has an idea
which stone
should receive second hand
dead flowers

she said she thought
she'd find a random grave
I say, pretty sure you don't want
to lay these on just any random
dead white man, she says right
those motherfuckers
may have owned slaves

I ask if I may offer a suggestion
she agrees. the monument
for the Arsenal Explosion
rests at the back edge of the yard
a memorial to seventy-eight
mostly twenty something
mostly Scotch and Irish women
who died making ammunition
in the worst
industrial accident
of The Civil War

she says perfect
as she lays a dead flower
on some random veteran's stone
a thought for her boyfriend
now serving in Afghanistan

I lead her to the far perimeter
stand aside
she studies the names
reads the inscriptions
walks around the stone
reaches in the bag
slowly
leaves and petals fall

-Baldinger

Lower

Dark far corner,
behind the pool table,
the video golf and
Deer Hunter games,
opposite the bathrooms,
no one comes by,
no one notices.
That's what he wants.

The air is stiff and hot
Even the bare bulb above
his booth has expired,
leaving him,
pickled though he may be,
the liveliest thing,
really the last living thing,
in that corner of the world.

As the reluctant waitress
brings him another
bottom shelf triple,
he muses on the virtue of
lowered expectations.

-Benger

Duke's Upper Deck Cafe

I finish the last swallow
of my second beer
leave a five spot
on the chrome
top of the bar
hold my teeth
as I step out
to the cold

the air is woodsmoke
there's a strange red
to the night

I focus my eyes
on the abandoned
space between buildings

if you breathe deeply
you still smell
the blood
turned molten
pouring
into ingots

-Baldinger

Nothing

He knew there'd be these nights,
but the intellectual cold
doesn't bite the core
as hard as the real thing.

The rain has been constant;
started long before
the sky went full black.

Wind from every direction
pulls at his will to continue,
a greedy lover
keeping him from life.

Nearly no cars pass,
and the ones that do
spray gutter water up his legs.

Every now and then
the gods decide upon
momentary light,
crack open the darkness,
illuminating everything
in strobe flashes of
horror movie despair.

He was sure he could do this,
but nights like this
make him wonder
how many more
nights like this
will pull him to the bottom,
send him back,
and it will all be
nothing.

-Benger

A River on Fire

reclamation of a faint crowd
the barmaid deals in time
it seemed like she was just doing
summer things, now it's winter again

I agree, April was a second ago
I was standing
in a parking lot watching
snowflakes disappear
into the waves
Lake of the Ozarks

today I'm on loop
circling four counties
I spent twenty minutes
staring at a painting
of a dead boy
shipwrecked
stood over by two men
a stringer of fish
on one of their shoulders

I don't know how to explain this
so, I tell her I'm driving
I'm from Pittsburgh
she makes it sound
as if it were century away

if I remembered the future
I'd say instead
I'm looking for Guan Yin

there's a song from 1989
in my head, I remember
that was the year my mother remarried
I remember an acre
of the yard completely covered
in a huge flock of crows
I remember my brother and I watching
Young Guns every day of August

hold the last lights
I caught a glimpse
of Joe Magarac, he bends steel
in front of a wall of memory
lost in the soot and dark smoke
the muted colors
of this city's past

there are dreams we forget
but then, we forget so much
more each time we wade
into a river on fire

-Baldinger

Mr. Petty

I had this English teacher in high school,
started mid-year.

Only reason I remember Mr. Petty's last name is:
on his first day,
after introducing himself,
first thing he said to us was:
No, I ain't related to
Richard or
Tom;
if I was,
I sure as shit
wouldn't be hangin around
with you little bastards.

Mr. Petty had
long hair and
a stud in his left ear.

Mr. Petty always smelled like
stale tobacco
and staler pot.

In the cafeteria,
Mr. Petty would let out
the most heinous
beer belches.

Mr. Petty's eyes were
perpetually half closed.

Mr. Petty had
a serious chip on his shoulder.

Mr. Petty moved from Florida,
cause this was the
only job he could find.

Mr. Petty was working on a novel,
workshopped it with the class once.
Had something to do with
drug deals on the docks
in Key West.
Protagonist's name was Kelly.
Kelly was a less than
thinly veiled Mr. Petty.

Once, Mr. Petty assigned us
an essay about anything.
Other kids,
they wrote about their dogs,
their girlfriends/boyfriends,
the homecoming game.
I turned in a paper
comparing and contrasting
Black Sabbath and Aerosmith.

Mr. Petty gave me the only A,
insisted I write an abstract,
and read it to the class.

When I told Mr. Petty
I wouldn't be around after Christmas break,
was moving to Kansas City,
he said:
Well, I hate to see you go,
but love to see anyone
get the fuck outta this town.

Sometimes I still think of Mr. Petty,
his long hair
and slacker breath.
His dreams of
being a famous novelist.
I hope he's doing okay,
maybe sold that novel.
I hope he's not still
obviously hating life,
going through the motions
teaching English to high schoolers in
a nothing town
in western Indiana.

-Benger

Beauty is a Rare Thing

on the back deck
of a civil war farmhouse
that survived gated in Pimlico
you pulled out these perfectly
rolled joints, the Reverend ran
into the woods to make water
on abandoned washer dryer combos

we watch the ghosts of owls
in an ancient walnut tree, you tell
me of your wife's affair, your daughter
and the relationship you struggle
to keep together. Fritz the cat
sprays the basement floor
all your art piled up/ forgotten
age and time passing
depression its own hair trigger

I've heard it said
beauty is a rare thing
it seems my artist friends
know this and fear this equally
we scatter to document it
we post it where we can
proof this whole fucking human
experiment isn't completely
futile

that night we read in your shop
to six people, we ate in some
shitty bar in the Inner Harbor
you felt you had outlived yourself
depression pulled you in
I'm never sure you got back out

that night I couldn't sleep
I got lost in the painting
in the dining room
flipped through myriad
books of photography
thinking on all our
faulty human prayers

after a couple years
I saw you again
friends heard
you were struggling
we came to watch
baseball, talk records

I spent the evening djing
while friends raided every room
trying to get you to sell
impossibly rare lps

after all these years
working around music

I see it like paintings
like poems, like sculpture
as something you can't truly
own, we pass it, accept it
it feeds us as we abandon
it to memory

I saw with each record
a look, painful
wash your face
you didn't understand
couldn't accept these things
were the sum of your legacy

after that the depression
pulled you back I didn't
see you again, social media
tells me this mortal coil
finally shook you, I hope
somehow as you found
the end to this life
that life finally
gave you some peace

                -Baldinger

Rot

The days crawl on
with a monotonous rapidity.

That she wouldn't mind so much,
but it's the ball of acid
that leeches from her guts
to everything,
eyeballs and fingertips,
lips and soul.

It tells her as it burns,
Nothing,
nothing,
no.

Just once
she would like to hear the
bright glowing affirmative
come from inside,
the cooling comfort
of internal approval.

The alarm blares hell.

As every morning,
she stares at the ceiling,
holds her breath,
hopes that today won't be
like all the others.

-Benger

Postcard from a Sunday Morning

the only cashier under sixty
at the rite aid looks hungover
I remind her I don't need a bag
as her chipped gold enamel
fingers fumble to open plastic

men wear reimagined
star wars t-shirts
in the laundromat
looking Sunday morning
rough, riding
some nostalgia trip
they rush through
try to complete
their task, before
mothers and feral
children take over

my left turn signal
spasms, doing its best
to remind that the bulb is out
I still forget

I play the same song
from 1993 over

and over, it was
a hit then, I dunno
if it's nostalgia
or a conjuring
I'm looking for

-Baldinger

Shelter

And then that night
when the cold,
the wet, the dark was
too much,
he found himself
with a full, warm stomach,
lying on a cot,
listening to her story.

She didn't want to do it,
you see?
But maybe that's not
all the way true;
she knew somewhere in there,
somewhere down,
the place where that deep tissue
is red and throbbing,
synapses fired,
and her spine went electric
when that hammer fell
the last time.

She tells him these things
as he lies uncomfortably comfortable,
tells him that's why
the jail,

and the parole,
and the jail again,
and the rehab,
and now here.

He does his best not to judge;
a general rule that's
kept him on the road to him
for a long time.

Still,
he doesn't sleep much
that night in the shelter,
and when he does,
it's shallow, with
dreams of the
nearest exit.

-Benger

The Ballad of Dominic Ierace

when my mother's second marriage
dissolved she spoke mostly in dreams
we were grown, still she wanted
to take us to Disneyland
she wanted to buy a house
she wanted to keep us safe
after six years of mostly volatile
rarely easy peace

she was forty something
working two jobs
circling the drain

I was barely twenty
working two jobs
circling the drain

neither of us could
afford a house alone
she asked me to cosign

after the Jaggerz broke a massive
hit with the *Rapper*
Dominic Irace changed his name
had a few big hits regionally

with a band called The Cruisers
if you live in Pittsburgh
you hear *Ah! Leah* or
Love is Like a Rock
as regular as *Stairway to Heaven*

in the mid-nineties Irace
wrote mortgages
rock star life
confined to weekend warrior status

I recognized him
didn't care
never star struck
not by rock stars
not by mortgage brokers
he's professional, goofy
till my mom steps out

at the copy machine
his posture changes
he's relating to me now
like he still wants to be remembered
as king cool, copier light glows
green, he shakes his head
says *it's a bitch, man*

                    -Baldinger

Cross-Dimensional

Another day
I wish you were
still here.

He ran
so fast,
wrestled with Pete;
he was the
perfect uncle,
you would've been
so proud.

I saw Dad
in his easy chair,
watching the mischief,
but imagined two chairs,
your clasped hands
bridging the negative space.

I wish you were here
to see your grandson;
he's just the little imp
you would've loved.

I miss you every day, Mom,
but sometimes I
see you in his eyes,
and those are the days
I hug him
just a little tighter.

When I do,
can you feel it?

-Benger

For Endless Summer

horizon starts to soften
I'm exhausted after ten
plus miles on the trails
shoes off, walk the breakers

there's a murder of crows
laughing at a surfer
who keeps biting in the waves

far off
in open water
a cruise ship
fades

two women
flash yoga poses
for a camera

two lovers
cuddle on a blanket
their intimacy watched
by a gull

two more
at the far edge
of the beach
sit quietly

the surfer gives up
bobs in the waves

I climb into a high back
chair of rocks
crack a warm beer
cheers the sky
for endless summer

-Baldinger

Sliver

And around noon,
coming out of a
wholly unrestful sleep,
she sees a sliver of
atomic white
peeking through,
as if forcing the curtains slit
by the sheer blinding force of
its unblemished purity.

There are days
when she wants to
run to the window,
yank the heavy drapes open
with everything her
slender arms will allow.
But it's all she can do,
rise to a slump,
shuffle to the wall,
inch the them back shut again.

That one sliver of light
burned acid with its
white hot promise,
the thought of being

fully exposed to it
makes her shudder,
with fear or excitement,
she's not sure.
But maybe the two are
more than just
not mutually exclusive.

-Benger

Lee's Famous Fried Chicken

Josh works the counter
at Lee's Famous Fried Chicken
he's got long, stringy hair
no front teeth, he compliments
my Bowie shirt, says it's his favorite lp

Dorsey and I take a booth
Josh is wiping down tables
he's got a bow and arrow
tattoo on his left calf
a primitive line drawing
perhaps a prison tattoo

he asks how the food is
says he's worked here nine years
he loves his job
his favorite is the two thigh meal
with red beans and rice
and macaroni and cheese
he says sometimes he gets
the biscuits and the apples
if you mix them together
you get a poor man's apple cobbler

-Baldinger

Life

About once a month or so
on one of her days to watch us,
Grandma would load us
into her 1975 Buick,
blue as all the oceans
I'd only seen in books.

No rule about seatbelts in Grandma's car;
they were just another
hippy conspiracy.
We'd bounce around the backseat
and watch the mysterious orange glow
of the cigarette lighter.

We'd make it to the mall;
wall to wall ads for all we wanted,
all we didn't need,
most we wouldn't have.

We'd walk
and walk
and walk.
Now having a child,
I understand these outings;

it was simply to tire us out.

Once she bought us a big soft pretzel
to share,
and the sweet memory of that rare treat
continues to linger.

If we were good,
we'd get a quarter a piece;
one chance to hone our
Centipede or Dig Dug skills.

As we left,
there was a penny-operated
helicopter ride.
We never got the penny,
but that didn't stop us
from hopping in,
pretending we were in
Air Wolf.

Afterward, us on the edge
of little kid meltdown,
Grandma'd take us to the
Bob Evans on the other side
of the parking lot.

A booth seat,
a carafe of coffee for her,
milk in Styrofoam cups
with lids and straws for us.

Complementary biscuits
as the waitstaff waited for a
food order that would never come,
containers of sugary, sticky plasma
on the table,
Grandma'd make us
honey and syrup sandwiches,
while shoving packets of
non-dairy creamer into her purse.
She didn't even put cream in her coffee,
but by God, if it was free,
it was going to be taken.

She'd return us to our
single-wide in the sticks,
holes in the floor and
outhouse in the backyard
in time for our parents
to deal with
sugar high toddlers.

Dad hung a special shelf
on the faux wood paneled wall
for Teddy Ruxpin to sit
and read me stories
until I finally succumbed to
the darkness outside the
cracked bedroom window.

One time a frog hopped up,
latched onto that window,
the noise, the foreign amphibian
freaked me to tears.
Dad came in,
told me that Mom
(who was working closing
at the Pizza Hut in town)
was working with God,
and they sent that frog
to watch over me while I slept,
and I believed it.

Life was Goddamned beautiful.

-Benger

This Drunk Apparition

as kids
we would race
we would fight
our way to the refrigerator
to grab cold bottles
of beer for my dad
his brother, their friends

we each knew
the tax system
we got the first swig
from the long neck
usually powered down
on the way to delivery

sometimes we would wait
vultures
looking for unattended bottles
to sneak another pull

it's summer
I'm extra hands
mostly beer runner
while my dad
and a neighbor
patch concrete steps

idle hands
versus
working hands

idle hands
keep grabbing
at the bottle
little fizz
shines down
my throat

floating
my father drops trowel
reaches for his beer

there is no sweat
left on the neck
there is no amber
in the vessel

I am a rubber band
caught and guilty
bubbling in the august night

he sends me home
I stumble the couple doors
back. my mother, grandmother
playing games on the porch

horrified at this drunk apparition
send me straight away
to bed, I go dry mouth
into that strange
rapid alcohol slumber

in the morning
lids peel from eyes
the ceiling is real estate
a sky pressing
hard on my forehead
my legs wobble
stomach backflips

a hangover
before it can be verbalized
is more like a dying butterfly

-Baldinger

today

this world
definitely now
but probably
always
has a way of
bringing us down
holding us there
making us
smell the dirt

constant reminders of
hopelessness

in the middle of this
the little girl
reaches for the
elderly man
says
i love you grandpa

clouds
moved on
today

-Benger

Midnight Prayer

with the night darker than any I've seen
with more stars than I may ever know
with the roar of the Atlantic filling my right ear
with the sounds of the forest night whispering in my left
with every cell of my being
                        receding
                              into
                                    nothingness

-Baldinger

James Benger is a father, husband and writer. His work has been featured in several publications. He is a member of the Riverfront Readings Committee, is on the Board Of Directors of The Writers Place in Kansas City, and is the founder of the 365 Poems In 365 Days online poetry workshop and is Editor In Chief of the subsequent anthology series. He lives in Kansas City with his wife and children.

Jason Baldinger is a poet hailing from Pittsburgh who recently finished a stint as writer in residence at the Osage Arts Community. He is co-director of The Bridge Series reading series, the author of several books including *This Useless Beauty* (Alien Buddha Press), *The Ugly Side of the Lake* (Night Ballet Press) written with John Dorsey, and *Little Fires Hiding* (Kung Fu Treachery Press) written with James. The collection *Fragments of a Rainy Season* (Six Gallery Press) is forthcoming. Recent publications include the *Low Ghost Anthology Unconditional Surrender, The Dope Fiend Daily, Outlaw Poetry, Uppagus, Lilliput Review, Rusty Truck, Dirtbag Review, Red Eft Review, In Between Hangovers, Your One Phone Call, Winedrunk Sidewalk, Anti-Heroin Chic, Nerve Cowboy Concrete Meat Press, Zombie Logic Press, Ramingo's Porch, Rye Whiskey Review, Red Fez, Mad Swirl, Blue Hour Review, Mojave River Review, Cajun Mutt Press* and *Heartland! Poetry of Love, Solidarity and Resistance*. You can hear Jason read poems on recent and forthcoming releases by Theremonster and Sub Pop Recording artist The Gotobeds as well as at jasonbaldinger.bandcamp.com

www.ingramcontent.com/pod-product-compliance
Lightning Source LLC
Chambersburg PA
CBHW020127130526
44591CB00032B/554